"I can fool you because you're a human. You have a wonderful human mind that works no different from my human mind. Usually when we're fooled, the mind hasn't made a mistake. It's come to the wrong conclusion for the right reason."

—Jerry Andrus, Magician

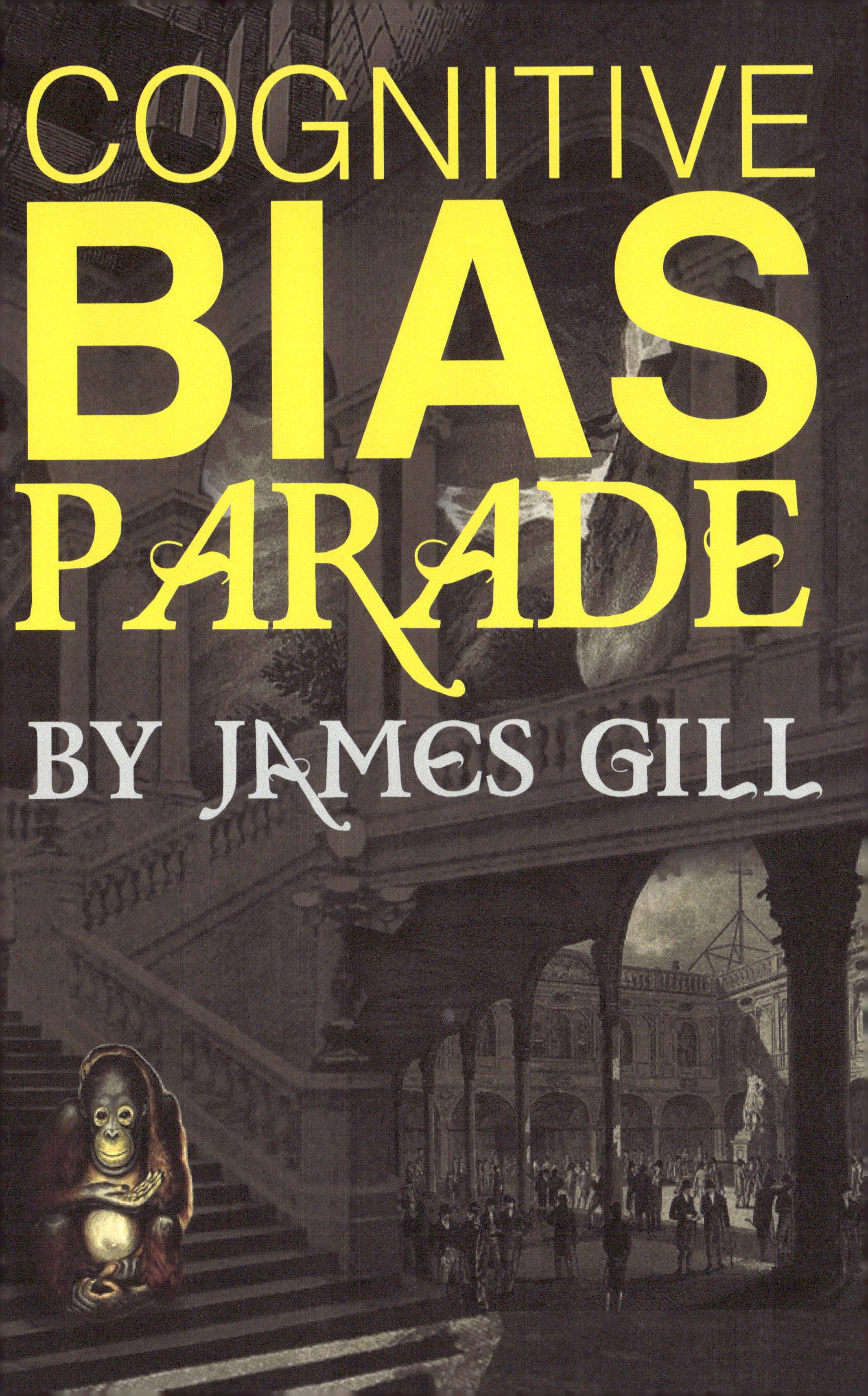

COGNITIVE
BIAS
PARADE

BY JAMES GILL

Cognitive Bias

A cognitive bias is a pattern of misjudgment in which people construct their own mistaken "subjective social reality".

Cognitive Biases can serve an evolutionary purpose, often enabling faster decisions when timeliness is more valuable than accuracy.

They also serve as the basis for almost all of the human comedy . . .

Dunning–Kruger effect

Incompetent people fail to realise they are incompetent because they lack the skill to distinguish between competence and incompetence.

cognitivebiasparade.com - Illusory correlation

Inaccurately perceiving a relationship between two unrelated events.

Illusory correlation

Inaccurately perceiving a relationship between two unrelated events.

Illusion of Control

is the tendency for people to overestimate their ability to control events, for instance to feel that they control outcomes that they demonstrably have no influence over.

Pareidolia

A vague and random stimulus (often an image or sound) is perceived as significant, e.g., seeing images of animals or faces in clouds, the man in the moon, and hearing non-existent hidden messages on records played in reverse.

13

cognitiveBiasParade.com | Rhyme as reason effect

Rhyme as reason effect

Rhyming statements are perceived as more truthful.

Illusion of transparency

People overestimate others' ability to know them, and they also overestimate their ability to know others.

Observation selection bias

The effect of suddenly noticing things that were not noticed previously – and as a result wrongly assuming that the frequency has increased.

Tip of the tongue phenomenon

When a subject is able to recall parts of an item, or related information, but is frustratingly unable to recall the whole item. This is thought an instance of "blocking" where multiple similar memories are being recalled and interfere with each other.

osterior bones, or digital ossicles of t

beyond these is the dark carbonize

lf of the fin, the outline of which

. t

b;

ina

ensuite du fumet de ces vers

Irrational escalation

is the phenomenon where people justify increased investment in a decision, based on the cumulative prior investment, despite new evidence suggesting that the decision was probably wrong. Also known as the sunk cost fallacy.

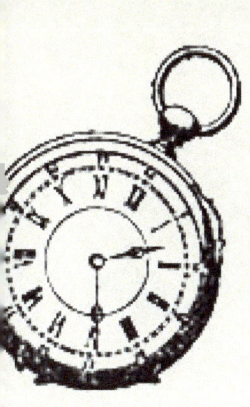

Planning
Fallacy

is the tendency to underestimate how long it will take to complete a task.

Apophenia

is the experience of seeing patterns or connections in random or meaningless data. Also, in 2008, Michael Shermer coined the word "patternicity", defining it as "the tendency to find meaningful patterns in meaningless noise".

Hindsight Bias

also known as the I knew-it-all-along effect or creeping determinism, is the inclination to see events that have already occurred as being more predictable than they were before they took place.

Confirmation Bias

Everything you seek
and all that you perceive
has away of proving
whatever you believe.

(also called confirmatory bias or myside bias)
is the tendency of people to favor information
that confirms their beliefs or hypotheses.

Functional Fixedness
affects the few
who forget that a function
can often be new.

Functional fixedness

limits a person to using an object only in the way it is traditionally used.

A simple lie told once, may not be well received,
but tell the lie a thousand times and it will be believed.

Availability cascade

is a self-reinforcing process in which a collective belief gains more and more plausibility through its increasing repetition in public discourse (or "repeat something long enough and it will become true").

Spotlight effect

The tendency to overestimate the amount that other people notice your appearance or behavior.

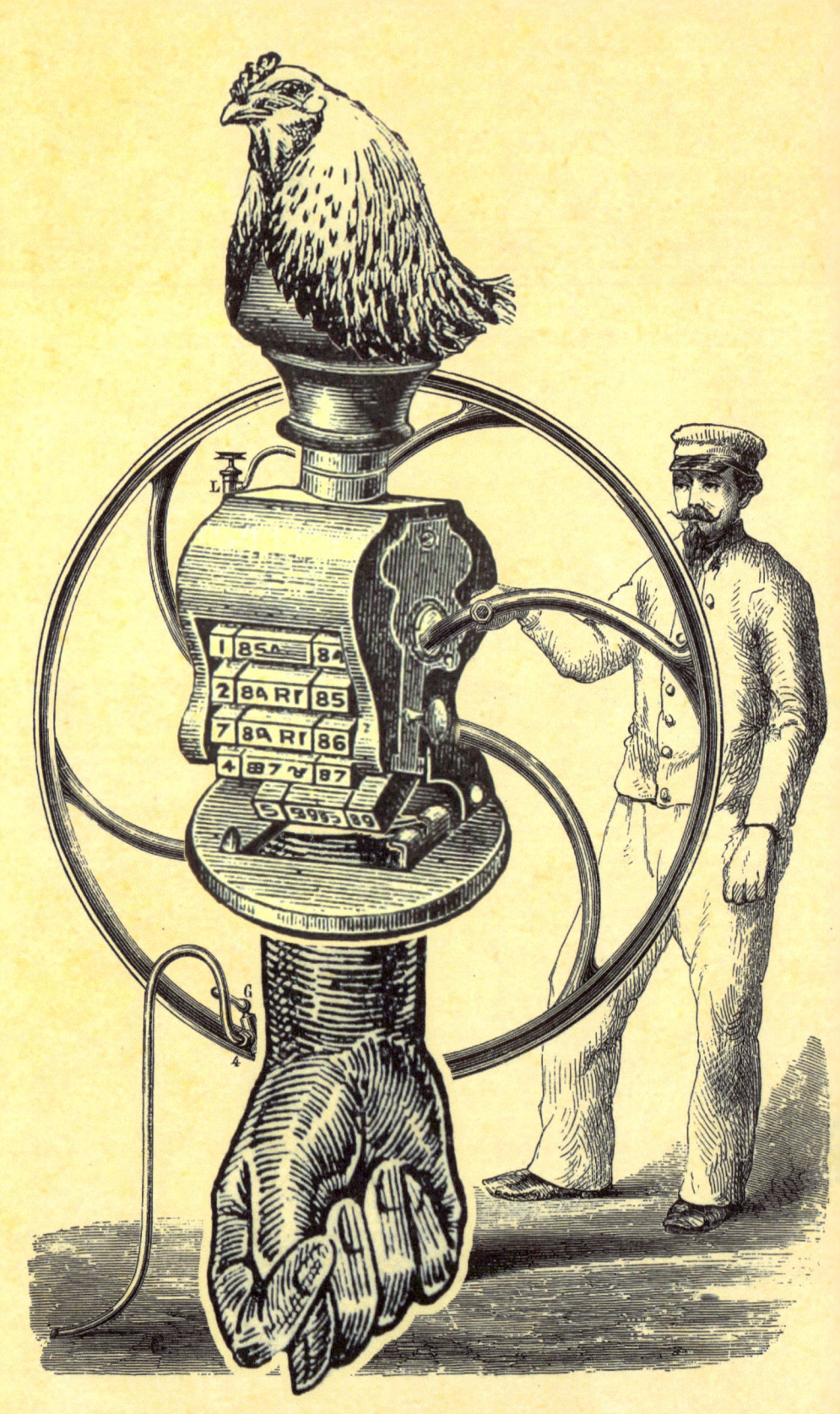

Post Purchase Rationalization

is a cognitive bias whereby someone who has purchased an expensive product or service overlooks any faults or defects in order to justify their purchase. It is a special case of choice-supportive bias.

Unit Bias

The tendency to want to finish a given unit of a task or an item. It has a strong effect on the consumption of food in particular.

Anchoring Effect

is a cognitive bias that describes the common human tendency to rely too heavily on the first piece of information offered (the "anchor") when making decisions.

Choice Supportive Bias

The tendency to remember one's choices as better than they actually were.

Availability Heuristic

lla gentile Sig.ra
:stefano, Via Roma 121
Catania

is the tendency to overestimate the likeli-
hood of events with greater "availability" in
memory, which can be influenced by how
recent the memories are or how unusual or
emotionally charged they may be.

KOZMATA

Ispund, emellan axlarne en bredd af 30 tum, armarnes längd är 40 tum.

About the author

James Gill is an artist and writer who lives in a house made of books, deep in the woods of southern Washington.
He shares the house with an old friend and one cat.

Elk, bears, rabbits and beavers prefer to live outside the house, which seems to suit everybody just fine.

www.ingramcontent.com/pod-product-compliance
Lightning Source LLC
Chambersburg PA
CBHW040326010626
45792CB00024B/2170